Music Superstars

BEYONCÉ

BY ARIEL FACTOR BIRDOFF

TORQUE

BELLWETHER MEDIA · MINNEAPOLIS, MN

Torque brims with excitement perfect for thrill-seekers of all kinds. Discover daring survival skills, explore uncharted worlds, and marvel at mighty engines and extreme sports. In *Torque* books, anything can happen. Are you ready?

This edition first published in 2025 by Bellwether Media, Inc.

Library of Congress Cataloging-in-Publication Data

Names: Birdoff, Ariel Factor, author.
Title: Beyoncé / by Ariel Factor Birdoff.
Description: Minneapolis, MN : Bellwether Media, 2025. | Series: Music superstars | Includes bibliographical references and index. | Audience: Ages 7-12 | Audience: Grades 4-6 | Summary: "Engaging images accompany information about Beyoncé. The combination of high-interest subject matter and light text is intended for students in grades 3 through 7"-- Provided by publisher.
Identifiers: LCCN 2024047000 (print) | LCCN 2024047001 (ebook) | ISBN 9798893042610 (library binding) | ISBN 9798893043587 (ebook)
Subjects: LCSH: Beyoncé, 1981--Juvenile literature. | Singers--United States--Biography--Juvenile literature. | LCGFT: Biographies.
Classification: LCC ML3930.K66 B57 2025 (print) | LCC ML3930.K66 (ebook) | DDC 782.42164092 [B]--dc23/eng/20241008
LC record available at https://lccn.loc.gov/2024047000
LC ebook record available at https://lccn.loc.gov/2024047001

Editor: Elizabeth Neuenfeldt Designer: Josh Brink

Printed in the United States of America, North Mankato, MN.

TABLE OF CONTENTS

HUMAN DISCO BALL!

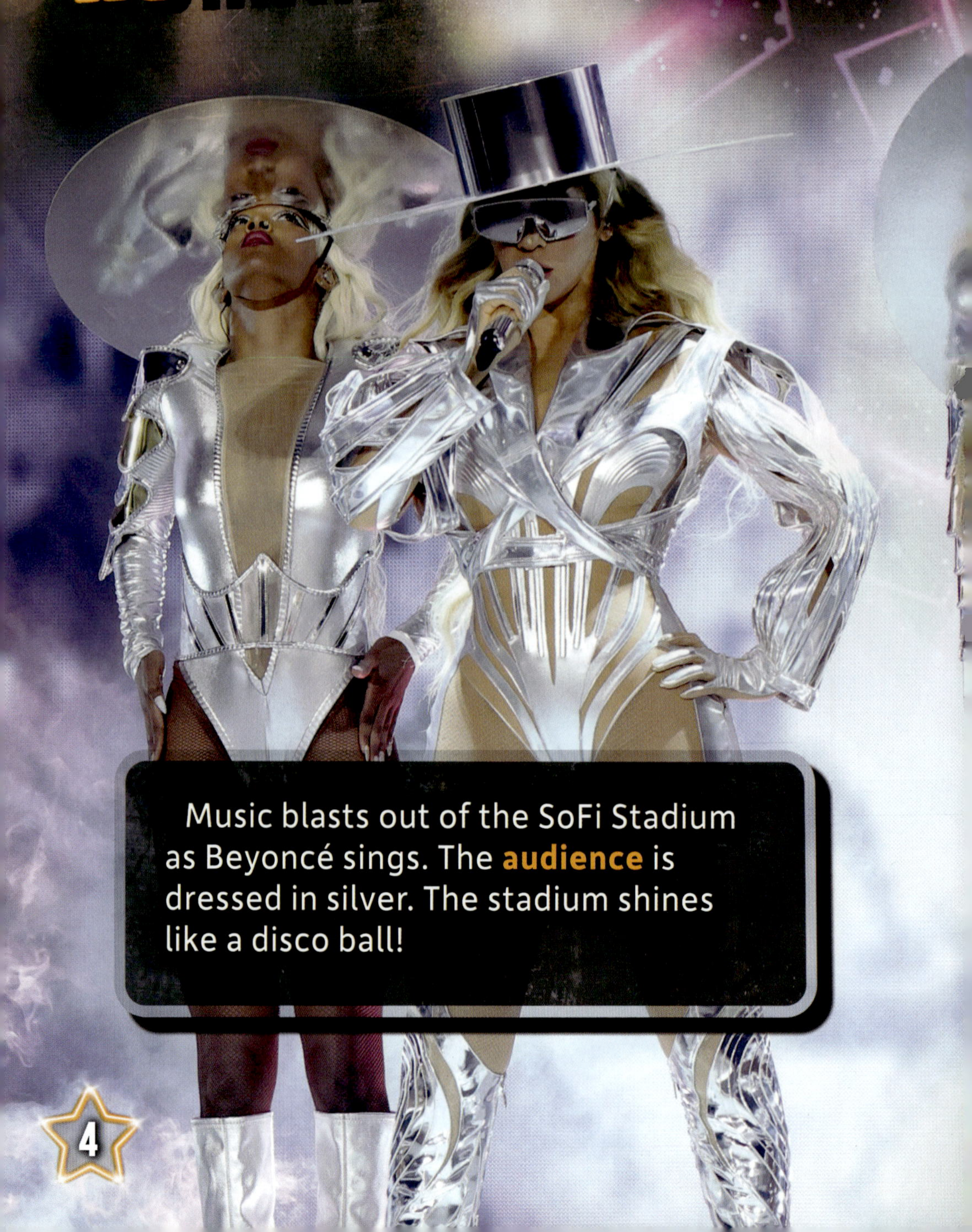

Music blasts out of the SoFi Stadium as Beyoncé sings. The **audience** is dressed in silver. The stadium shines like a disco ball!

This 2023 Renaissance World Tour show closes as Beyoncé sings "Summer Renaissance." She rises up over the crowd on a silver horse. Fans cheer for this record-breaking singer!

WHO IS BEYONCÉ?

Beyoncé is a famous singer and songwriter. She sings R&B and many other types of music. As of 2024, she has made eight **solo** albums.

2023 GRAMMY AWARDS

BEYONCÉ

Birthday	Hometown	Types of Music	First Solo Hit
September 4, 1981	Houston, Texas	R&B, soul, pop, country	“Crazy in Love”

Some of her hit songs include “Crazy in Love” and “Single Ladies.” Beyoncé has won many awards. She has 32 **Grammy Awards**. That is more Grammys than any other artist!

FOLLOW YOUR DREAM!

Beyoncé Giselle Knowles was born on September 4, 1981. She grew up in Houston, Texas, with her family. When Beyoncé was 7, she won her school's talent show. She beat classmates more than twice her age!

SINGING SISTERS

Beyoncé's sister Solange is also a singer and songwriter!

SOLANGE

At age 9, she formed a band with her friends. The band was called Girl's Tyme. Beyoncé was the lead singer.

Girl's Tyme began singing and dancing in contests. In 1992, the group entered one of the United States' most popular television talent shows called *Star Search*.

DESTINY'S CHILD

FAVORITES

Singer
Stevie Wonder

Food
pizza

Ice Cream
butter pecan

Number
four

Sadly, Girl's Tyme did not win. In 1996, the band changed its name to Destiny's Child. Their luck was about to change, too.

FROM BAND TO SOLO

Destiny's Child worked with Columbia Records. They **released** albums and singles. Some of the biggest hits were "Say My Name" and "Independent Women Part I."

In the early 2000s, Beyoncé wanted to make her own music. Destiny's Child took a break. In 2003, Beyoncé released her first solo album, *Dangerously in Love*. It **debuted** at number one on the ***Billboard*** 200!

MOVIE STAR!

Beyoncé's first movie appearance was *Carmen: A Hip Hopera*. It aired on MTV in 2001.

Beyoncé's first hit single was "Crazy in Love." The song was one of her first **collaborations** with rapper Jay-Z. It won two Grammys!

TOP COLLABORATOR

Beyoncé has worked with many artists. She has worked with artists such as Shakira, Lady Gaga, Dolly Parton, and Miley Cyrus!

JAY-Z

AWARDS

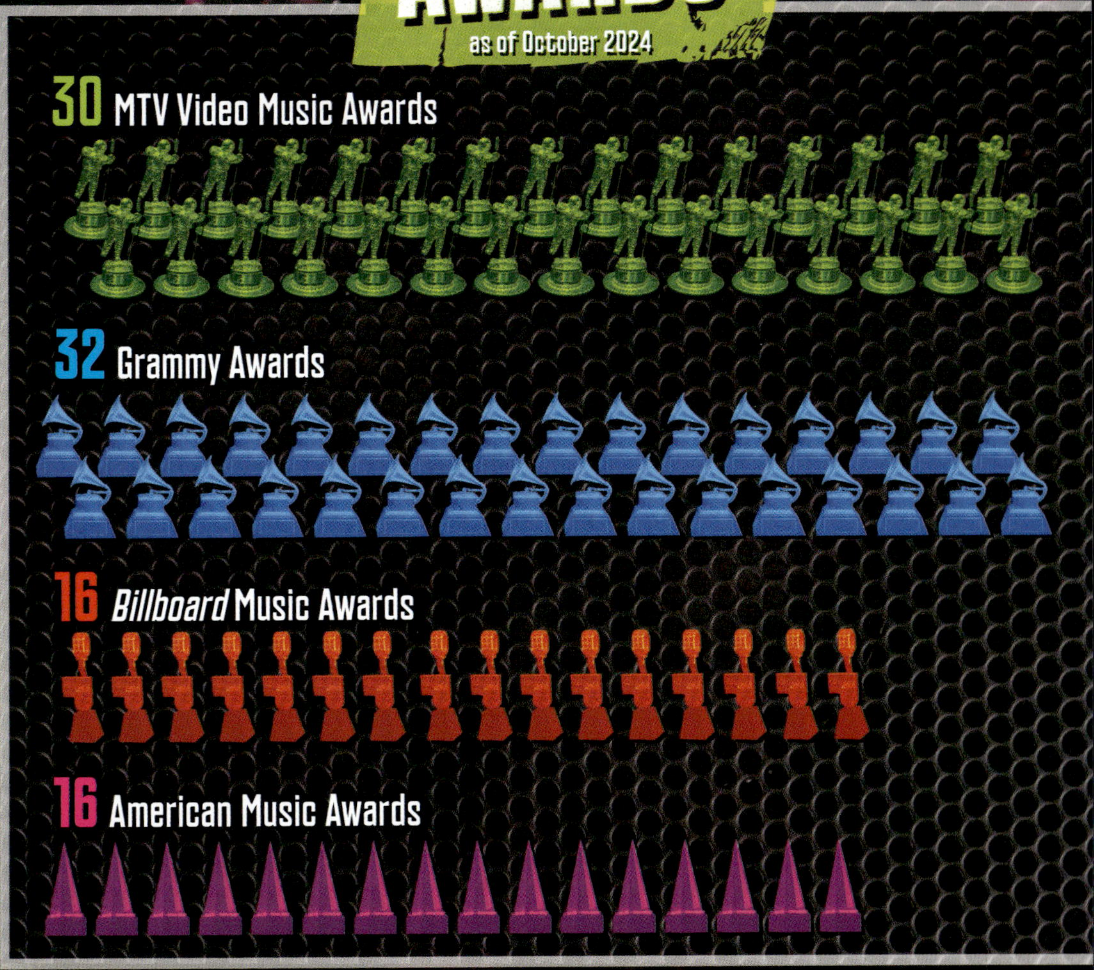

In 2006, she released the album *B'Day*. It was a hit! Two years later, she made *I Am... Sasha Fierce*. In 2010, Beyoncé won six Grammys and got her first Album of the Year **nomination**.

Her album 4 came out in 2011. Fans loved it! The album *Beyoncé* released in 2013. *Lemonade* released in 2016. These hit albums talk about **feminism**.

2013 SUPER BOWL PERFORMANCE

Beyoncé's albums were successful. She earned two more Album of the Year nominations at the Grammys. She also sang at the Super Bowl Halftime Show in 2013 and 2016!

Renaissance came out in 2022. Beyoncé was the first solo artist to have their first seven studio albums debut at number one in the U.S.! In 2023, she became the artist with the most Grammys!

In 2024, Beyoncé released the country album *Cowboy Carter*. She became the first Black woman to top the *Billboard* Top Country Albums chart!

TIMELINE

– 1990 –

Girl's Tyme forms

– 2003 –

Beyoncé's first solo album is released

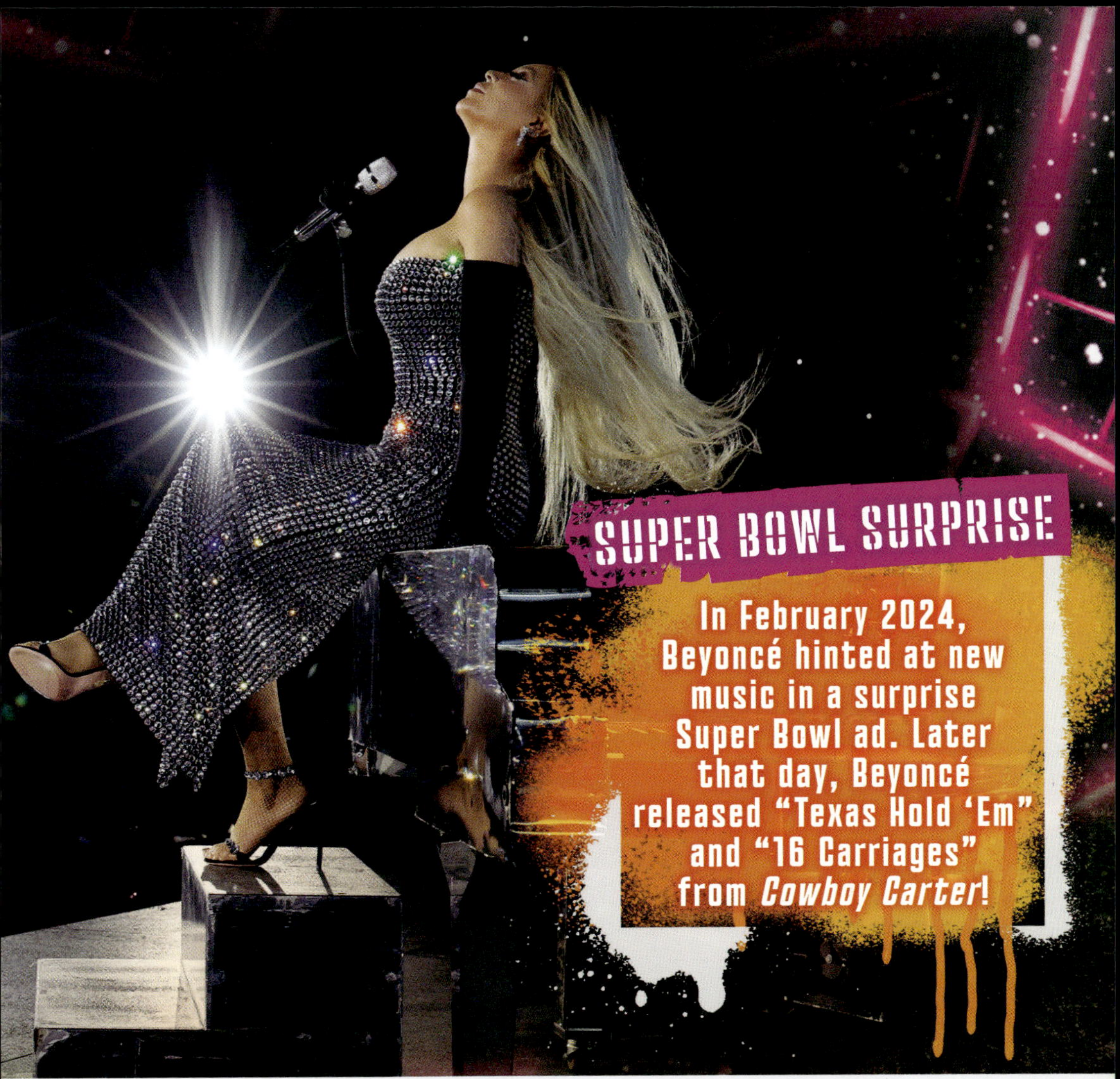

SUPER BOWL SURPRISE

In February 2024, Beyoncé hinted at new music in a surprise Super Bowl ad. Later that day, Beyoncé released "Texas Hold 'Em" and "16 Carriages" from *Cowboy Carter*!

–2013–

Beyoncé performs at the Super Bowl Halftime Show

–2023–

Beyoncé becomes the artist with the most Grammy Awards

–2023–

Beyoncé becomes the first Black woman to top the *Billboard* Top Country Albums chart

THE BEYHIVE!

Beyoncé is known as Queen Bey. Her widespread and loyal fans are called the Beyhive. When Beyoncé asked her hive to dress like a human disco ball for the end of her Renaissance World Tour, they were happy to do it. The results were amazing!

PLAYLIST

"Crazy in Love"
(2003)

"Halo"
(2008)

"Single Ladies"
(2008)

"Run The World (Girls)"
(2011)

"16 Carriages"
(2024)

BUZZ, BUZZ

Bey is pronounced like the word "bee."

The world cannot wait to see what Queen Bey will do next!

GLOSSARY

audience—a group of people watching a concert

Billboard—related to a well-known music news magazine and website that ranks songs and albums

collaborations—things created while working with others

debuted—was introduced or released for the first time

feminism—the belief that all genders are equal

Grammy Awards—yearly awards given by the Recording Academy of the United States for achievements in music; Grammy Awards are also called Grammys.

nomination—the process of being chosen as a candidate for an award

released—made music available for listening

solo—relating to music performed by one person

TO LEARN MORE

AT THE LIBRARY

Lavette, Lavaille. *Beyoncé: A Little Golden Book Biography*. New York, N.Y.: Penguin Random House, 2023.

Vegara, Maria Isabel Sanchez. *Beyoncé*. London, U.K.: Frances Lincoln Children's Books, 2024.

Wilkins, Ebony Joy. *Beyoncé: Queen of the Spotlight*. New York, N.Y.: Penguin Random House, 2020.

ON THE WEB

FACTSURFER

Factsurfer.com gives you a safe, fun way to find more information.

1. Go to www.factsurfer.com.
2. Enter "Beyoncé" into the search box and click 🔍.
3. Select your book cover to see a list of related content.

INDEX

The images in this book are reproduced through the courtesy of: Raph_PH/ Wikipedia, front cover (Beyoncé); Taya Ovod, pp. 2-3; Kevin Mazur/ Getty Images, pp. 3, 4-5, 7 (main, infographic), 18-19, 20, 21, 23; Las Vegas Review-Journal/ Getty Images, p. 5; Chris Pizzello/ Invision/ AP Newsroom, p. 6; Julia Reinhart/ Getty Images, p. 8; NC1/ WENN/ Newscom, p. 9; STAR SEARCH, Ed McMahon/ Everett Collection, p. 10; Houston Chronicle/ AP Newsroom, pp. 10-11; Dorota Szymczyk, p. 11 (Stevie Wonder); Mad-Max7, p. 11 (pizza); Riju959, p. 11 (ice cream); Patrick Krabeepetcharat, p. 11 (4); Rob Watkins/ Alamy, p. 12; Dave Hogan/ Getty Images, pp. 12-13; KMazur/ Getty Images, pp. 14-15; WFDJ_Stock, p. 11 (MTV Video Music Awards); CarlosVdehabsburgo/ Wikipedia, pp. 15 (Grammy Awards), 19 (Grammy Award); Kathy Hutchins, p. 11 (*Billboard* Music Awards); s_bukley, p. 15 (American Music Awards); Charles Sykes/ AP Newsroom, p. 16; Patrick Semansky/ AP Newsroom, p. 17; jbrink, pp. 18 (album), 21 (playlist); Dabarti CGI, pp. 18-19 (timeline mixing board).